This Bing book belongs to:

....

Copyright © 2024 Acamar Films Ltd

The *Bing* television series is created by Acamar Films and Brown Bag Films
and adapted from the original books by Ted Dewan.

The Leaf Hunt is based on the original story 'Leaf Pictures' written by Nicky Phelan, Mikael Shields and Claire Jennings.
It was adapted from the original story by Lauren Holowaty for HarperCollins *Children's Books*.

HarperCollins *Children's Books* is a division of HarperCollins*Publishers* Ltd
1 London Bridge Street, London SE1 9GF

www.harpercollins.co.uk

HarperCollins*Publishers*
Macken House, 39/40 Mayor Street Upper, Dublin 1, D01 C9W8

1 3 5 7 9 10 8 6 4 2

ISBN: 978-0-00-861957-2

Printed in Malaysia

This book is produced from independently certified FSC™ paper
to ensure responsible forest management.

For more information visit: www.harpercollins.co.uk/green

THE LEAF HUNT

HARPERCOLLINS
CHILDREN'S BOOKS

Round the corner, not far away,
Bing is in the woods today.

"Neooooowwww!"

"C'mon, Sula!" calls Bing,
running through the woods with his friends.

Amma finds a picnic table and everyone gathers round. "Okay, you noisy bangers," she says. "Who's ready to be an artist today?"

"Oo! Me!" shout Bing, Sula and Pando.

"I'm a quality artist," says Coco.

First they need to find special autumn leaves for their pictures. "Ready?" asks Amma. "Off you . . ."

"Go, go, go, go, gOOOOO!" they all cheer.

Everyone looks for their leaves in the woods.

"BROWN! Found one!" says Pando, holding up his curly leaf.

"That's an OAK leaf from an oak tree," explains Sula. "Oak trees have curly leaves."

"Oh, I love this red one!" says Sula, picking up a beautiful red leaf.

"Oooh! An orange one!" says Bing. But as he tries to pick it up . . .

. . . the wind blows the leaf down the woodland path.

Whoosh!

"Oh!" says Bing chasing after it. "Come back, leaf! Stop it, wind!"

Bing manages to stop the leaf with his foot.

"Well done, Bing," says Flop.

Bing holds it up. It's bright orange and curly.

"Ta-da!" cheers Coco, as she shows everyone a **rainbow-coloured** leaf.

"That's a **sycamore** leaf," says Sula.

"It's red, orange, yellow and green!" says Coco. "It's the most **special** leaf ever!"

"Wow!"

Amma calls everyone back to the picnic table
and tells them to lay their leaves down bumpy
side up, and put a sheet of paper on top of them.

"Next we choose a coloured crayon," says Amma. "Then, we hold the paper and gently rub the crayon over the leaf, like this . . ."

Swoosh-roosh-swoosh-roosh!

As Amma rubs the crayon, all the lines from the leaf show through the paper, making a beautiful leaf picture!

Everyone copies Amma to
make their own leaf pictures.

"Oh!" says Bing, excited to see his leaf shape
coming through. "Look at my leaf, Flop!"

Whoosh!

The wind lifts up Bing's picture. **"Come back, leaf,"**
he says, holding it down to stop it from flying away.

"Good catch, Bing!" says Flop.

"Finished!" says Pando, proudly holding up his picture before searching for another leaf.

"Oh wow, wasn't that fast?" says Amma.

"I'm going to make mine a
real rainybow leaf!" says Coco.

"But there aren't *really* rainybow leaves,"
says Sula looking up at the trees.

"When you're being an artist," explains Amma,
"you can make your picture ANY way you like."

"Pando, can I have the purple crayon?" asks Coco.
But as she reaches for the crayon, the wind
blows her picture off the table.

Whoosh!

"Oh!" says Bing, seeing Coco's picture flying off.
He jumps up and steps on it to stop it from going any further.

"BING!" shouts Coco. "You **stamped** on my picture!"

"Oh . . . erm," says Bing, seeing his muddy footprint on Coco's rainybow leaf.

"It's **ruined** now!" says Coco.

Bing whispers, "No . . . I was trying to save it . . . And Coco, you are *angry*."

Amma goes over to Coco and gently asks,
"What happened, Coco?"

"Bing **stamped** on my picture!" says Coco.

"Ohhh," says Amma.

"What happened, Bing?" asks Flop.

"Um, the wind blew Coco's picture
and I caught it for her," explains Bing.

"Well, that was kind, Bing," says Flop. "Do you think
Coco knows that you were **trying** to help?"

"Um . . . no," says Bing.

"I *did* stamp on your picture, Coco," Bing starts, "but . . . I'm SORRY you are angry."

"Maybe we all feel a bit angry, Bing, if someone messes our picture up," says Flop, "even if they *were* trying to help."

"Can you mess it down again?" asks Bing.

"We can't mess Coco's picture down," replies Flop, turning to Coco. "But sometimes a quality artist can see how to fix their picture up."

"I suppose," considers Coco. "I *am* a **quality artist.**"

Pando brings over a crayon and gives it to her. "You can have the purple now," he says.

Coco takes the purple crayon and looks at her picture thoughtfully. And then she has an idea!

Everyone sits back down at the picnic table and Coco starts to sing The Rainybow Song as she draws.

"Pretty purple, indigo . . ."

They all join in and start to pass Coco the colours she needs to finish.

". . . sliding down the rainybow!"

"Your foot's going to be a rainybow, Bing!" giggles Sula.

"Sunset orange, ruby red, rainybow above your head. That's the way the colours go, sliding down the rainybow!"

They finish singing and everyone claps.

"Yay!"

"Good for you, Bing Bunny," chuckles Flop. "And good for you too, Coco!"

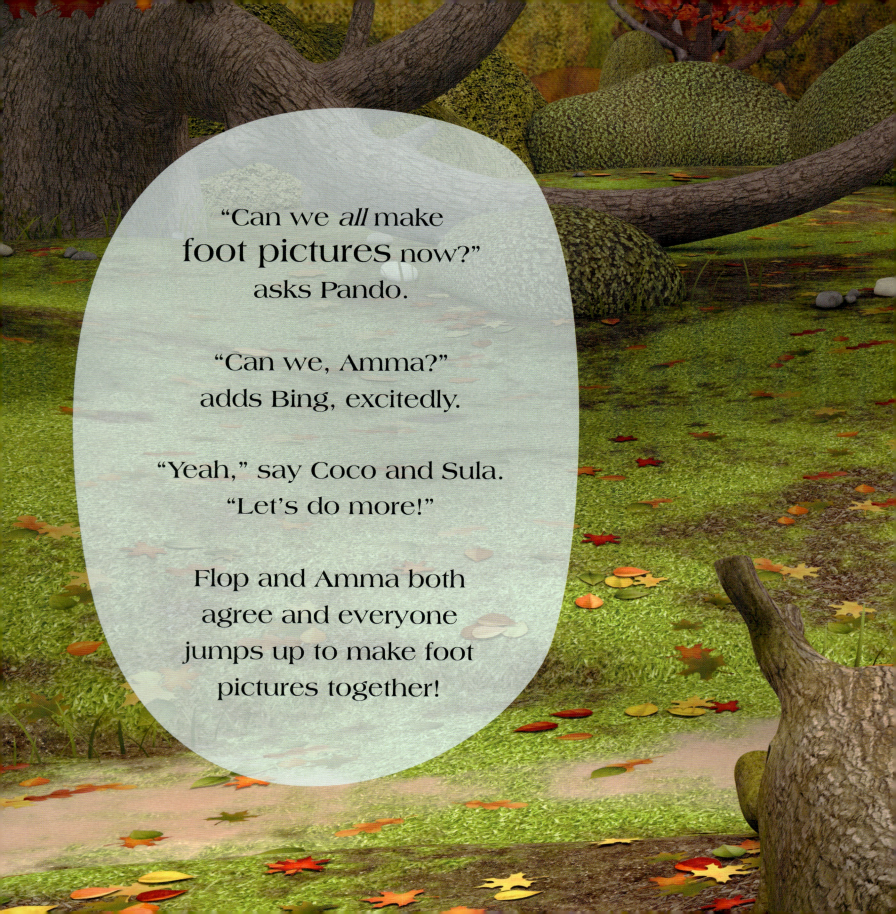

"Can we *all* make
foot pictures now?"
asks Pando.

"Can we, Amma?"
adds Bing, excitedly.

"Yeah," say Coco and Sula.
"Let's do more!"

Flop and Amma both
agree and everyone
jumps up to make foot
pictures together!

**Making pictures . . .
it's a Bing and Coco thing!**